A book to discover a child's imagination and knowledge

By Michael Smith

Cover art and book illustrations
by Albert Lin and Crystal Smith

•

Book design
by Albert Lin (Apococo Visual Image)

East West Discovery Press
Los Angeles

Text copyright © 2003 by Michael Smith
Cover art and book illustrations copyright © 2003 by Albert Lin and Crystal Smith

Published by:
East West Discovery Press
P.O. Box 2393, Gardena, CA 90247
Phone: 310-532-1115 / Fax: 310-768-8926

Editor: Gillian Dale
Treasure box illustration by Albert Lin
Children illustrations by Crystal Smith
Book design by Albert Lin (Apococo Visual Image).

First edition, April 2003
Printed in Korea. Published in the United States of America

Publisher's Cataloging-in-Publication
(Provided by Quality Books, Inc.)

Smith, Michael, 1961-
    Questions for kids : a book to discover a child's
  imagination and knowledge / by Michael Smith ; cover art
  illustration by Crystal Smith and Albert Lin ; book
  design by Albert Lin.
    p. cm.
    SUMMARY : Collection of stimulating questions designed
  to inspire young minds.
    LCCN 2002094728
    ISBN 0-9669437-1-6

    1. Imagination in children--Problems, exercises, etc.
  --Juvenile literature. 2. Creative thinking in children
  --Problems, exercises, etc.--Juvenile literature.
  [1. Creative thinking. 2. Imagination.] I. Title

BF723.I5S65 2003   155.4'133
                          QBI02-701999

ISBN 0-9669437-1-6 (Paperback)
ISBN 0-9669437-3-2 (Hardcover)

Books may be purchased in bulk or customized for promotional or educational purposes. Inquiries for foreign language translation, distribution, rights and permissions should be addressed to: East West Discovery Press, P.O. Box 2393, Gardena, CA 90247.
Printed in Korea

I wish to thank Professor Gillian Dale for editing this book, Julie Van Ryckegen for her thoughtful contributions, my loving wife Icy for turning the questions I ask our children, into this book and Crystal and Celena, our daughters, who are the sources of inspiration for this endeavor. May their future be bright and their happiness stay contagious.

INTRODUCTION

In our family, we have question time. Several times a week, as a game, my kids get asked 20 or 30 questions in a row. Many reasons to do this are obvious, but the main reason my kids ask to play this family game is because it's fun. You can do this too, and to get you started without taxing your brain with creating questions, here are some that have worked for us. In the car, at the park or at the grandparents' house, quality interaction with children can be easy.

In the development of a child's mind, nothing is more important than lots of questions. Kids have a built in sense of curiosity and ask you questions without prompting, but children need to be asked lots of questions, too. For them to simply memorize information is not enough. Kids need their curiosity stimulated and their powers of deduction challenged. High-achieving adults are often those who have been asked lots of questions when they were kids. Ask your child lots of easy questions now, and the hard questions will come easier later on.

Some words of advice before you start:

☐ **M**odifying some questions will be necessary. For example, for an older child, change "Name three colors" to "Name eight colors". We have used outlined fonts in our questions to highlight words that can easily be changed to form similar questions, either simply to add variety or to make the question easier or harder.

☐ **C**hoose questions the child can easily answer correctly some of the time, but not all of the time. Try for a balance between confidence-building, easy questions and harder ones; many learning opportunities can come from questions answered incorrectly and the explanations they will prompt.

☐ **C**arefully responding with corrections is important. When the answer is wrong, give detailed answers to some interesting questions, but provide only quick answers to most others to keep your child's interest. A check mark ✓ on incorrect answers can allow you to return later to try again.

☐ **A**dd your own question to follow-up on an answer that was thought-provoking. For example, "What would you do if a stranger offered you some candy?" could be followed by "What would you do if a stranger said 'Hi!'" Contrasts between two questions can make the child think even harder.

☐ **A**dding your own questions about the experiences they have had in recent memory can help establish the habit of reflecting on daily events.

☐ **F**or kids at similar levels, a competition of who can answer first is a great game.

☐ **F**or more than one child, take turns back and forth with age-appropriate questions. Read the question to yourself; then modify it to the particular child's ability and don't be afraid to skip hard ones if the child gets more than a few wrong in a row. Remember that the outlined words are easy for the questioner to vary.

☐ **E**nglish as a Second Language students of any age can have fun practicing their English too.

☐ **A**bove all, learning should be fun! Never use this book against the child's will. Try to cut off your questions before they are tired. Let them beg for a few more, in a mild way, and encourage their interest next time.

The information a child can learn from the questions in this book and the habits of thinking that will be strengthened are of great value, but the interaction between you and the child may be even more rewarding. You can learn where the child is developmentally, and the child can learn your values.

Now your family has a powerful educational tool that is fun for all -- so enjoy!

○ **1**. What is the most important part of your body ?

○ **2**. Can you ride an airplane to the moon ?

○ **3**. How many sides does a closed box have ?

○ **4**. Does a mailman deliver email ?

○ **5**. Why do some snakes bite ?

A book to discover a child's imagination and knowledge

○ **6**. Why do you wash your hands before you eat ?

○ **7**. What flies in the air but never eats food ?

○ **8**. Can you count forever ?

○ **9**. What can you do to keep your teeth healthy besides brushing them ?

○ **10**. What pushes on kites to make them fly ?

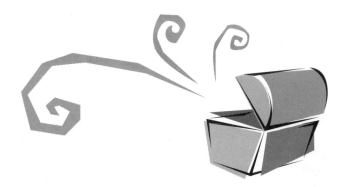

○ **11**. What are some ways you can help stop crime ?

○ **12**. How many days are there in a week ?

○ **13**. When is your birthday and how old will you be ?

○ **14**. Besides your lips, what part of your body do you need to blow up a balloon ?

○ **15**. What animal can swim and walk ?

○ **16**. What are eyebrows for ?

○ **17**. What would you do if you were scared of someone at school ?

○ **18**. Who are the people you love ?

○ **19**. What planet do you live on ?

○ **20**. If you have two dogs, three pencils and a bird, how many animals do you have ?

○ **21**. Is asking questions a good thing ?

○ **22**. What kind of pets do people have ?

○ **23**. What would you ride in if you were going across a lake ?

○ **24**. If you do not know what a word means, what would you do ?

○ **25**. How many letters are there in the alphabet ?

○ **26**. Name as many animal babies as you can. For example, baby cats are kittens.

○ **27**. What is a right way to ask for something ?

○ **28**. What are some of the things bridges cross over ?

○ **29**. Name some words that rhyme.

○ **30**. Where is the best place for monkeys to live ?

○ **31**.What should you eat to make your bones strong ?

○ **32**.Would you like to live in the forest ?

○ **33**.What animals would not make good pets ?

○ **34**.What are some things you need to do when you take care of a cat ?

○ **35**.What are clouds made of ?

36.How does it make you feel when it rains ?

37.What can happen if plants get too much water ?

38.Are cartoons ever real ?

39.Where does rain go after it hits the ground ?

40.What is the biggest animal you know ?

○ **41**. Do whales breathe air ?

○ **42**. Do fish breathe air ?

○ **43**. Do plants need air ?

○ **44**. Why is putting a bag over your head dangerous ?

○ **45**. What happens if you get too much sunshine ?

A book to discover a child's imagination and knowledge

○ **46**. Can you get too much love ?

○ **47**. What are rubber bands made of ?

○ **48**. Why is it necessary to cook some food ?

○ **49**. Why are ants interesting ?

○ **50**. What would you do if you have some cloth but no clothes ?

○ **51**. What would happen if you ate some food that went bad ?

○ **52**. What happens if you pee pee in the pool ?

○ **53**. What happens if it rains too much ?

○ **54**. What are your favorite things to do with your mom ?

○ **55**. Do some bats eat mosquitoes ?

○ **56**. What animals eat mice and rats ?

○ **57**. What food do vegetarians not eat ?

○ **58**. What do carnivorous animals eat ?

○ **59**. What do you eat ?

○ **60**. Where does fruit come from ?

○ **61**. What do you need to make a pizza ?

○ **62**. What would you do if someone were mean to you ?

○ **63**. Why should you be nice to others ?

○ **64**. What would happen if a plant does not get enough sunshine ?

○ **65**. If you have a question, who can you ask ?

○ **66**. Can you hear a picture?

○ **67**. Should you tell others about yourself, that you look pretty (handsome) ?

○ **68**. Should you tell others that you are smart ?

○ **69**. If your friend is smart, should you tell them ?

○ **70**. Are there some schools for cooking ?

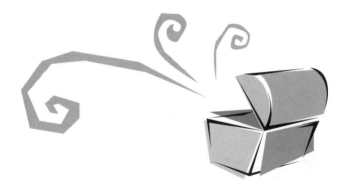

○ **71**. What is the blood in your body for ?

○ **72**. What are some kinds of pollution ?

○ **73**. Can you count backwards from 10 ?

○ **74**. What can you eat that never was alive ?

○ **75**. Does a plant have a heart ?

A book to discover a child's imagination and knowledge

○ **76**. When is breaking a rule okay ?

○ **77**. Where would you go if there were a hurricane or tornado ?

○ **78**. How would you feel if someone stole something from you ?

○ **79**. What is the difference between an island and a lake ?

○ **80**. What do both planes and birds have ?

○ **81**. What can cause smoke ?

○ **82**. Why do people need love ?

○ **83**. What does a bird do to fly ?

○ **84**. What is the opposite of hot ?

○ **85**. Is there anyone who never
makes mistakes ?

○ **86**. Name some animals that have tails.

○ **87**. What kinds of things would you see in a park ?

○ **88**. Which is sweeter, honey or lemons ?

○ **89**. What do you say if someone does something for you ?

○ **90**. How can you get germs off your hands ?

○ **91**. How many tires do three cars have ?

○ **92**. What makes a car go ?

○ **93**. Name three things that come from clouds.

○ **94**. Why should you not eat paper ?

○ **95**. Name three things you can do with a computer.

96. If you have one dollar and someone gives you another eight dollars, how many would you have ?

97. Who do you like to hug ?

98. Can loud music hurt your ears ?

99. Name three animals you can ride on.

100. What is your favorite thing to do in the morning ?

○ **101**. Are dinosaurs real ?

○ **102**. Are there any dinosaurs alive today ?

○ **103**. What is your favorite weather ?

○ **104**. What do you and dogs have in common ?

○ **105**. What do you and snails have in common ?

106. Should a child take medicine without help from an adult ?

107. What time will it be two hours from now ?

108. What are some different kinds of art ?

109. What are some of the differences between boys and girls ?

110. Are all girls smarter than boys ?

111. Are all boys taller than girls ?

112. Name something that is not real but some people think is real.

113. Will talking to a plant help it grow ?

114. Is listening to the teacher important ?

115. If you have three cups of water and you pour out one, how many cups of water do you have ?

A book to discover a child's imagination and knowledge

116. Can bugs eat a whole dead animal ?

117. What happens to a body after it dies ?

118. Does different skin color make people smart or dumb ?

119. Name two different religions.

120. Do you know any other religions ?

○ **121**. What is the biggest
number you can think of ?

○ **122**. What is the next biggest
number after the biggest
one you could think of ?

○ **123**. What would you need to dig
a big hole ?

○ **124**. Why do you close the door
if the air conditioner or
heater is on ?

○ **125**. Is all money green ?

A book to discover a child's imagination and knowledge

○ **126**. Ask a question that has no answer.

○ **127**. What is ketchup made from ?

○ **128**. What grade will you be in two years from now ?

○ **129**. Are some rules no fun ?

○ **130**. Can you make something move just by looking at it ?

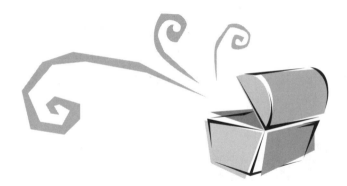

131. Can dogs and cats eat some 'people food' ?

132. If you could change one thing in the world, what would it be ?

133. In a magic trick, when something disappears, is it really gone ?

134. Who are your ancestors ?

135. What are some of the things people do differently today than they did a long time ago ?

A book to discover a child's imagination and knowledge

136. Why should you never stick something in your ear ?

137. What are some of the rules you have at school ?

138. What kind of art can you do ?

139. Is it okay to look at the sun ?

140. What are some of the things that belong to *you* ?

○ **141**. What can kids do to make money ?

○ **142**. What are some things that can get you in trouble ?

○ **143**. What is a nice thing you can do for somebody ?

○ **144**. Did you ever do something very dumb ?

○ **145**. Are you smart ?

A book to discover a child's imagination and knowledge

○ **146**. Should you always try your best ?

○ **147**. If you could fly, where would you go ?

○ **148**. Close your eyes. What color clothes am I wearing ?

○ **149**. With your eyes still closed, what colors are you wearing ?

○ **150**. Imagine you are in the water. What kinds of things would you see ?

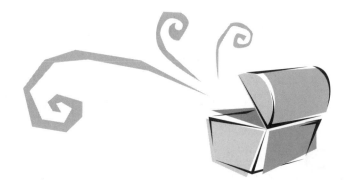

O **151**. Imagine you are in a very old house. What kinds of things would you see ?

O **152**. Make up a short song and sing it.

O **153**. Did all the dinosaurs die before people evolved ?

O **154**. What would you do if you were very scared of something you dreamed about ?

O **155**. If you think about something good before you sleep, will you dream about something good ?

○ **156**. Name something you can do to keep yourself healthy.

○ **157**. Do you want to make other people happy ?

○ **158**. If you were a parent, would you punish a child if he or she made a bad mistake ?

○ **159**. What would you do to punish kids for bad behavior ?

○ **160**. Are kids usually shorter than their parents are ?

○ **161**. Would you forgive kids for most mistakes ?

○ **162**. Would you do your homework even if your parents did not ask you to do it ?

○ **163**. Is any spice not spicy ?

○ **164**. What do you have as part of your body that monkeys do not have ?

○ **165**. Who are your grandparents ?

○ **166**. Would you like to go into space ?

○ **167**. What does the earth look like from space ?

○ **168**. Is a star bigger than the earth ?

○ **169**. If you wanted to tell someone something, but you could not speak, what would you do ?

○ **170**. If you pointed up, would someone on the other side of the earth think that direction is down ?

○ **171**. Name something that is not alive.

○ **172**. Where is a good place to find answers to questions about animals ?

○ **173**. What is so good about books ?

○ **174**. How do you say 'thank you' in Spanish ?

○ **175**. What does a red stoplight tell you to do ?

○ **176**. What kind of birds do you know ?

○ **177**. Is there any bird that can't fly ?

○ **178**. What birds swim in the ocean ?

○ **179**. Are there any fish that can fly ?

○ **180**. Can some people live forever ?

o **181**. What are some of the things you can do with feathers ?

o **182**. Where do your parents work ?

o **183**. If you like someone, what can you do to show it ?

o **184**. Spell some words that have five letters.

o **185**. Name three organs that are inside your body.

○ **186**. What does the organ in your body called the liver do ?

○ **187**. What part of your body allows you think ?

○ **188**. Why does some food go in the refrigerator ?

○ **189**. What do plants eat ?

○ **190**. What are some different ways you can cross a river

○ **191**. Is there any tree that can talk ?

○ **192**. What do Chinese people eat with ?

○ **193**. Can anyone learn to use chopsticks ?

○ **194**. If you have eight pencils, and you give two to your mom, and three to your dad, how many will you have left ?

○ **195**. What do some people use to see better ?

○ **196**. Why do dogs bark ?

○ **197**. Which moves more slowly, a snail or a grasshopper ?

○ **198**. What do you do if a big dog gets in the way of where you are walking ?

○ **199**. Why do people go to work ?

○ **200**. What would it be like if the tires on a bicycle or car were made of something hard instead of rubber ?

○ **201**. What is school for ?

○ **202**. Should you drink ocean water ?

○ **203**. What should you do if there is an earthquake ?

○ **204**. What should you do if someone has very bad breath ?

○ **205**. Is there more ocean or land on earth ?

A book to discover a child's imagination and knowledge

206. What are three ways you can stay dry when it rains ?

207. How many minutes are there in an hour ?

208. What do monkeys and you both like to eat ?

209. What is the biggest thing you can think of ?

210. How do you spell your full name ?

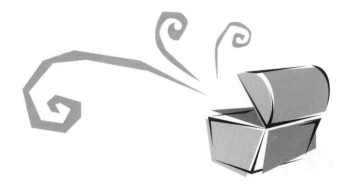

○ **211**. Spell your first name backwards.

○ **212**. How old were you three years ago ?

○ **213**. Name something that makes light but does not use electricity.

○ **214**. What is the smallest thing you can think of ?

○ **215**. What is the tallest thing you can think of ?

A book to discover a child's imagination and knowledge

○ **216**. If you have three grapes, four pencils and a banana, how many pieces of fruit do you have ?

○ **217**. What is your favorite vegetable ?

○ **218**. Do all fish have bones ?

○ **219**. What is music for ?

○ **220**. Do snails have bones ?

○ **221**. Name two animals that live in a shell.

○ **222**. Should you always do what someone older tells you to do ?

○ **223**. Can you name all the months in the year ?

○ **224**. Does an eight-year-old child always know more than a seven-year-old child ?

○ **225**. What do police do ?

A book to discover a child's imagination and knowledge

226. What would happen if you fell into a frozen lake ?

227. What would happen if everyone littered ?

228. Why should you eat food that is good for you ?

229. Do fish have feathers ?

230. What would you do if the driver of a car fell asleep while driving ?

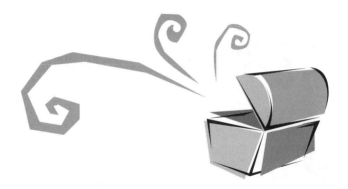

○ **231**. What animals have feathers ?

○ **232**. Where do you like to go on field trips ?

○ **233**. What places are hot ?

○ **234**. What letters (called a prefix) can you put in front of a word to make it mean the opposite ?

○ **235**. What do pilots do ?

○ **236**. Does a duck have lips?

○ **237**. What keeps a bird in the air ?

○ **238**. What language do people in Japan speak ?

○ **239**. How far can you count in Spanish ?

○ **240**. How many nickels are there in a dime ?

241. How many legs do one spider and one octopus have all together ?

242. Why shouldn't kids play with matches ?

243. How many toes and fingers do three people have ?

244. How many hours are there in a day ?

245. How many seconds are there in a minute ?

A book to discover a child's imagination and knowledge

○ **246**. Are monsters real ?

○ **247**. How many straight lines does it take to draw a door ?

○ **248**. What animals besides cows produce milk ?

○ **249**. Name some seeds that are good to eat, and some that are not good to eat.

○ **250**. What do you do if a stranger gives you something nice and asks you to come with them ?

○ **251**. Why do you sleep ?

○ **252**. Why does a doctor give immunization shots ?

○ **253**. What does an artist do ?

○ **254**. What kinds of art do not have pictures ?

○ **255**. Name some different kinds of music.

○ **256**. Is drinking water good for you ?

○ **257**. Why do you go to school ?

○ **258**. What shape is your planet ?

○ **259**. What shapes are the other planets ?

○ **260**. What shape is a box ?

○ **261**. Why do we need bees around fruit trees ?

○ **262**. Why do you want food to be cold ?

○ **263**. Name a vegetable that is orange.

○ **264**. What would happen if you did not throw away garbage ?

○ **265**. What is the red liquid in your body ?

A book to discover a child's imagination and knowledge

○ **266**. Name the vowels.

○ **267**. What would you do if you found a gun ?

○ **268**. What city do you live in ?

○ **269**. Name some foods that grow on trees.

○ **270**. What are some fruits that you can not eat ?

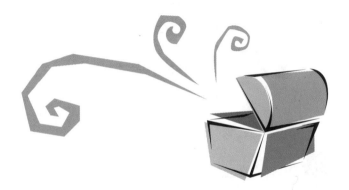

○ **271**. What besides a bicycle has two wheels ?

○ **272**. If you want to talk to someone and they are already talking to someone else, what should you do ?

○ **273**. How many months are there in a year ?

○ **274**. What do you do before eating and after using the restroom, and why ?

○ **275**. What are the bones in your body for ?

○ **276**. What country do you live in ?

○ **277**. What does a porcupine use to protect himself ?

○ **278**. What do you do before you cross a street ?

○ **279**. What are seat belts for ?

○ **280**. If you get cold at night, what should you do ?

281. What kind of food is green on the outside and red on the inside ?

282. What do you want to be when you grow up ?

283. If you have a green banana, what do you do to make it yellow ?

284. What is the difference between a sailboat and a motor boat ?

285. Can you name three musical instruments ?

○ **286**. What is the oldest thing you know ?

○ **287**. What language do they speak in England ?

○ **288**. Can you name seven vegetables ?

○ **289**. How can you make music if you have no musical instruments ?

○ **290**. If food has been sitting out for a long time, why can't you eat it?

291. What do air conditioners do ?

292. What do you need if you go camping in the mountains ?

293. What kinds of things live under ground ?

294. What two things will ice turn into if you cook it ?

295. What makes a tree grow ?

A book to discover a child's imagination and knowledge

○ ***296***. What makes kids grow ?

○ ***297***. Why should you never take someone else's medicine ?

○ ***298***. Are gorillas almost like people ?

○ ***299***. Is the water in most lakes salt water ?

○ ***300***. When are your family members' birthdays ?

○ **301**. What phone numbers do you know ?

○ **302**. What number do you dial to get the police or ambulance ? When would you use it ?

○ **303**. How does a letter you mail get to where it is going ?

○ **304**. What are postage stamps for ?

○ **305**. Do you know anyone from another country ?

306. What customs do they have in that country that are different than those in your country ?

307. Where do your grandparents live ?

308. How would you describe yourself over the phone to someone that you do not know so that they could recognize you when they meet you ?

309. How would you describe yourself to someone so they will understand more about you than what you look like ?

310. Name eight things that live in the ocean.

○ *311.* How many stars are there ?

○ *312.* What is something you and
plants both need ?

○ *313.* What do you do if your
knee is bleeding ?

○ *314.* What sport uses a pig skin ?

○ *315.* Why are flowers colorful ?

○ **316**. Name five things you would need a ticket for.

○ **317**. How many thumbs do 14 people have ?

○ **318**. What do you call babies born on the same day from the same mother ?

○ **319**. Why should you save some of your money ?

○ **320**. Which is bigger, a thousand or a hundred ?

○ **321**. What does fur do for animals ?

○ **322**. What do cars drive on ?

○ **323**. Where does the market get the vegetables they sell ?

○ **324**. Do people live on other planets ?

○ **325**. What is a star ?

○ **326**. What do you do if someone in your house looks sick and will not wake up ?

○ **327**. Name some insects.

○ **328**. Name five different kinds of plants.

○ **329**. What do you do if you are in bed and you get cold ?

○ **330**. If there are six blankets and two beds, how many blankets should each bed get ?

○ **331**. What do you do if you get separated from your parents in the mall ?

○ **332**. What does the sun give us ?

○ **333**. What language is spoken in Mexico ?

○ **334**. Name as many countries as you can.

○ **335**. If you had rings on all of your fingers but not your thumbs, how many rings would you have on one hand ?

○ **336**. Are there more than a hundred hairs on your head ?

○ **337**. Are there more than a billion ?

○ **338**. Which is more important: to get all the answers right, or to try your hardest ?

○ **339**. Is it good to run in a store ?

○ **340**. How many corners does a square has ?

○ **341**. What do you do if you see someone steal something ?

○ **342**. How do cats clean themselves ?

○ **343**. What animal has wings but no tail ?

○ **344**. How much time is twice the time of six minutes ?

○ **345**. How many legs do four horses have ?

346. If it takes you two minutes to eat one piece of candy, how many minutes would it take you to eat two pieces ?

347. What does the green traffic light mean ?

348. If someone does not speak English, does that make him or her stupid ?

349. What will happen if you kiss a frog ?

350. Is it easier to ride a bicycle up a hill or downhill ?

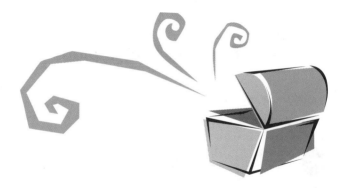

351. What is in the center of most fruit ?

352. How can you earn money ?

353. Name some people who work in hospitals and explain what they do.

354. When would you go to a hospital if you were not sick ?

355. What does a plant start as ?

○ **356**. Where do you put dirty clothes ?

○ **357**. Do all feathers come from birds ?

○ **358**. What is missing in the following ? 14, 15, 16, 18

○ **359**. What are the last three letters of the alphabet ?

○ **360**. If you have one noodle and you cut it in half, how many noodles do you have ?

○ **361**. If you have three ducks and one flies away, how many do you have left ?

○ **362**. What do you need to get your hands really clean, besides water ?

○ **363**. Name some parts of your head.

○ **364**. What do some people wear to hold up their pants ?

○ **365**. Why is telling the truth important ?

366. What room in your house is used to prepare food ?

367. Why don't you eat food that has been on the floor ?

368. What are three reasons to wear gloves ?

369. What animals are found on a farm ?

370. What language would you like to learn and why ?

371. Who are some of the important people in your life ?

372. What things need water to live ?

373. What do you use to cut paper ?

374. How many sides does a triangle have ?

375. How many corners does a circle have ?

A book to discover a child's imagination and knowledge

○ **376**. What do your muscles
need to be strong ?

○ **377**. How do you grow your
mind ?

○ **378**. What is paper made from ?

○ **379**. Where does wood come
from ?

○ **380**. What do trains ride on ?

381. What are the different ways you can get to San Francisco ?

382. What is a fire extinguisher used for ?

383. What would you need to move a hill ?

384. What do you need to make a sandwich ?

385. If a zebra had no stripes, what animal would it look like ?

○ **386**. What do fishermen use to catch fish ?

○ **387**. Do fish have brains ?

○ **388**. If there is a family with a mommy and a daddy and they have three children, how many people are there in all ?

○ **389**. Why do babies cry ?

○ **390**. Why do cows make milk ?

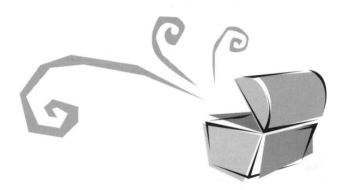

○ **391**. What sound does a cow make ?

○ **392**. What do bears use to keep warm ?

○ **393**. What can you make by sewing pieces of cloth together ?

○ **394**. What does thread come from ?

○ **395**. Name four things that are beautiful.

○ **396**. Where do cubs come from ?

○ **397**. Why do people laugh ?

○ **398**. How do you make a cake ?

○ **399**. Name six things that are living, and three things that are not living.

○ **400**. Is it a good idea to eat a bug ?

401. What do you need if you want to make a sign ?

402. Where does honey come from ?

403. What about stoves can be dangerous ?

404. What do you do if you are thirsty ?

405. What could happen if you drop a glass ?

A book to discover a child's imagination and knowledge

○ **406**. What should you do if someone tries to touch your private parts ?

○ **407**. What do you do if part of the house catches on fire ?

○ **408**. Are movies real ?

○ **409**. What do you do if you smell smoke when you are in bed at night ?

○ **410**. If one of your chickens lays four eggs and another chicken lays two eggs, how many eggs do you have in all ?

411. What is interesting about cultures other than your own culture ?

412. Why do you look both ways before crossing the street ?

413. Which is closer to your house, the moon or another country ?

414. What are the roots of a plant for ?

415. If you lose your leg in an accident, can you grow one back ?

○ **416**. Are there such things as evil spirits ?

○ **417**. Can you return to the past ?

○ **418**. Why is smoking bad for you ?

○ **419**. Do you want to be a parent someday ?

○ **420**. Where does rain come from ?

421. How many quarters are there in a dollar ?

422. If you walk in a big circle, where will you end up ?

423. If you have four half-full buckets of water, how many full buckets do you have ?

424. Name three things that would float if you put them in a swimming pool.

425. Name three things that would sink if you put them in a swimming pool.

A book to discover a child's imagination and knowledge

○ **426**. Name four liquids.

○ **427**. Name two gasses.

○ **428**. What is heavier, water or air ?

○ **429**. If you take a deep breath, would you float in water ?

○ **430**. Do all balloons go up in the air ?

○ **431**. Why do some balloons go up and some down ?

○ **432**. Is the gas in a balloon going up heavier or lighter than air ?

○ **433**. Is it possible to jump out of a flying plane safely ?

○ **434**. Can anyone float in the air ?

○ **435**. Why do monkeys and people look a little alike ?

○ **436**. Which is more important, trying hard or winning ?

○ **437**. What can you do to save forests ?

○ **438**. What can you do to conserve water ?

○ **439**. What does the saying, "Waste not, want not" mean ?

○ **440**. What is your nationality ?

○ **441**. What is your race ?

○ **442**. Are some races better
than others ?

○ **443**. What country did your
grandparents come from ?

○ **444**. Where did your ancestors
come from ?

○ **445**. How many eyes do five
people have ?

○ **446**. What do you do if your pencil gets dull ?

○ **447**. What kind of food do babies eat ?

○ **448**. What do plants eat ?

○ **449**. Where do the eggs we eat come from ?

○ **450**. Do any other animals produce eggs ?

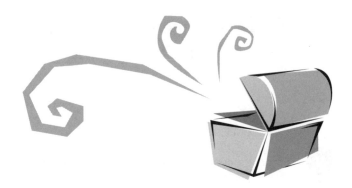

○ **451**. Is it good to try new things you haven't eaten before ?

○ **452**. What would you do if you found a lot of money ?

○ **453**. What happens if you eat a lot of junk food ?

○ **454**. Where does wool come from ?

○ **455**. Where does cotton come from ?

○ **456**. What can you make out of wool or cotton ?

○ **457**. What would happen if you ate too much every day ?

○ **458**. What would happen if you eat too little every day ?

○ **459**. If you were going to Japan, how would you get there ?

○ **460**. What are your toes for ?

○ **461**. What are some of the things you can do to help clean your house ?

○ **462**. Would you brush your teeth even if no one told you to ?

○ **463**. What are some ways you can learn new things ?

○ **464**. What do you need to open a lock ?

○ **465**. Is it okay to open the door if a stranger wants to give you something ?

○ **466**. What letters in the alphabet look the same upside down ?

○ **467**. Name some other things that look the same upside down.

○ **468**. What letter does the letter "M" look like upside down ?

○ **469**. What can you ride in that goes on a track ?

○ **470**. Does anyone look exactly the same as someone else ?

471. Name different kinds of clothes you can wear for school.

472. Name some animals that have horns.

473. If you change your socks every day and you have six pairs of socks, when will you run out of fresh socks to wear ?

474. What are some of the different languages people speak ?

475. What comes out of the radio that you can dance to ?

○ **476**. Can ladies grow a beard ?

○ **477**. If you had two extra fingers, how many fingers would you have all together ?

○ **478**. How many numbers are there on a clock ?

○ **479**. What do you put at the end of a sentence ?

○ **480**. How can you talk to someone who is far away if you can't go there ?

○ **481**. Is magic real ?

○ **482**. Why is exercising your body important ?

○ **483**. What comes after R in the alphabet ?

○ **484**. If you make a mistake with a pencil, what do you need to fix it ?

○ **485**. How many states border your state, and which ones are they ?

A book to discover a child's imagination and knowledge

○ ***486***. What should you do when you get your hands dirty ?

○ ***487***. What parts of your body do you use to read ?

○ ***488***. What are some of the things in your school room ?

○ ***489***. What kind of things can burn you if you are not careful ?

○ ***490***. Name something hard that you can see through.

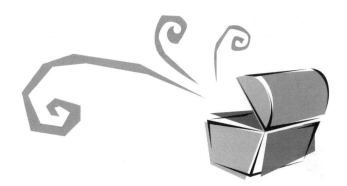

○ **491**. Name something soft that you can see through.

○ **492**. What do you need to breathe ?

○ **493**. What is the main thing that your body is made of ?

○ **494**. What sports do you like to play ?

○ **495**. Where does snow come from ?

○ ***496***. What is your favorite game ?

○ ***497***. What grows out of the top of a man's head ?

○ ***498***. Where can people learn another language ?

○ ***499***. Name three things that are good to sit on.

○ ***500***. What is a map for ?

○ **501**. Where do the toys at the market come from ?

○ **502**. Why are knives not toys ?

○ **503**. Why do trees have leaves ?

○ **504**. Where do flashlights get their energy ?

○ **505**. Name four different fruits.

○ **506**. What kind of sound does a cat make ?

○ **507**. Name two different kinds of meat.

○ **508**. Does anyone else have the same fingerprints as you do ?

○ **509**. Beef comes from what animal ?

○ **510**. Name four kinds of juice.

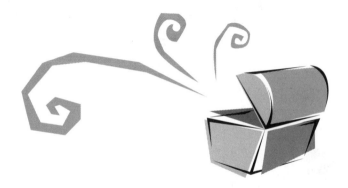

511. What kind of juice would never taste good ?

512. What things do you need to kiss ?

513. What is inside of a tire ?

514. What is inside of your lungs ?

515. Name three things that smell bad.

○ **516**. What can you say if someone sneezes ?

○ **517**. What does your heart do ?

○ **518**. What comes at the end of a sentence when it is a question ?

○ **519**. What part of your body tastes things ?

○ **520**. What is the main ingredient in candy ?

521. Where does sugar come from ?

522. Why does music make people feel good ?

523. What flies but is not a bird ?

524. What part of your body smells things ?

525. What should you do if your car is stuck on a railroad crossing ?

○ **526**. What does peanut butter come from ?

○ **527**. What do you need to buy things ?

○ **528**. How many legs do 11 people have ?

○ **529**. If you have eight dollars and you spend three, how many do you have left ?

○ **530**. Why do people sneeze ?

○ **531**. How many thumbs do 50 people have ?

○ **532**. Snow melts into what ?

○ **533**. How old can people live to be ?

○ **534**. Name four colors.

○ **535**. Name four things you can see in the sky.

○ **536**. How can you make a Popsicle ?

○ **537**. Spell your sibling's name.

○ **538**. Name some cities.

○ **539**. Does the color of someone's skin make them good or bad ?

○ **540**. What do you like best at school ?

○ **541**. Name three things that are not real.

○ **542**. Name three things that are good for you that you can drink.

○ **543**. Name five fruits.

○ **544**. What are the colors of a stoplight and what do they mean ?

○ **545**. What does dental floss do ?

○ **546**. Name four ways to make music.

○ **547**. What is the purpose of a park ?

○ **548**. Where does metal come from ?

○ **549**. What kind of sound does a dog make ?

○ **550**. Name three things that smell good.

○ **551**. What is missing: a fork, a knife and a _____ ?

○ **552**. What is next after 17, 16, 15, 14 ?

○ **553**. What shape has eight sides ?

○ **554**. If you want to cook, what are some of the things you will need ?

○ **555**. How many tires does a bicycle have ?

O **556**. Are chicken feathers good to eat ?

O **557**. What kinds of clothes do you wear in very cold weather ?

O **558**. What are windows made of ?

O **559**. What color is corn ?

O **560**. What does blood do in your body ?

○ **561**. What are teeth for ?

○ **562**. What is soap for ?

○ **563**. What are four ways to communicate ?

○ **564**. How many days are there in a month ?

○ **565**. What animals have no hair ?

○ **566**. What keeps the rain out of a house ?

○ **567**. What is inside your head ?

○ **568**. What do you want to be when you grow up ?

○ **569**. What does a tree start out as ?

○ **570**. What music do you like ?

○ **571**. Who are your friends ?

○ **572**. Where do seeds come
from ?

○ **573**. What does spicy food
taste like ?

○ **574**. Name seven things you can
eat that are not cooked.

○ **575**. Where does rain come
from ?

○ **576**. How many inches are there in a foot ?

○ **577**. Should you eat flowers ?

○ **578**. What happens to people who steal ?

○ **579**. What does a sailboat use for power ?

○ **580**. What does a car use for energy and power ?

○ **581**. What do kids use for energy and power ?

○ **582**. What can you eat that grows without any sunlight ?

○ **583**. What pumps blood in your body ?

○ **584**. Where does salt come from ?

○ **585**. What are rubber bands, balloons and tires all made out of ?

○ **586**. Where do mountains come from ?

○ **587**. When you jump up, what pulls you back down ?

○ **588**. Why do bees go to flowers ?

○ **589**. What bad thing could happen if you throw sand at someone ?

○ **590**. What are mirrors for in the car ?

○ **591**. What do you turn on to hear music ?

○ **592**. What do you do if you see someone steal something ?

○ **593**. Why do bees sting ?

○ **594**. If you want to be a doctor, what do you need to do ?

○ **595**. Why is it more dangerous for kids walking near cars ?

○ **596**. How many friends can you name from your school ?

○ **597**. What are some different ways to exercise ?

○ **598**. What can hold more people than three cars ?

○ **599**. How many straight lines does it take to make two triangles ?

○ **600**. Is it okay to run around where there are cars around ?

601. Name four animals and make the sounds they make.

602. What do you say if someone offers you drugs ?

603. How many days are there in a year ?

604. What do you look at to find out what time it is ?

605. Name three dangerous things that kids should not play with.

A book to discover a child's imagination and knowledge

○ **606**. Name three things that are polite to say.

○ **607**. Name three states.

○ **608**. What are books for ?

○ **609**. Where can you go to borrow books ?

○ **610**. Where can you buy books ?

○ **611**. Are books only for learning things ?

○ **612**. Are insects closely related to people ?

○ **613**. What animals are similar to people ?

○ **614**. What different kinds of foods are there in other countries ?

○ **615**. Is it good to meet people from other countries ?

○ **616**. What is the difference between a cellular telephone and a regular telephone ?

○ **617**. What do you hate ?

○ **618**. Is it okay to fight sometimes ?

○ **619**. Should you make fun of people who look strange to you ?

○ **620**. Do adults sometimes make mistakes ?

○ **621**. Name three birds you can eat.

○ **622**. Do you think people in other cultures may think you look and act strange ?

○ **623**. Can cleaning up be fun ?

○ **624**. Name a food you remember that you liked that was new to you.

○ **625**. Should you be friendly to new people you meet ?

○ **626**. Are some people unfriendly ?

○ **627**. What do good kids get if they are good ?

○ **628**. What are the initials for television ?

○ **629**. What are your initials ?

○ **630**. Name six words that began with "T".

○ **631**. Name an animal that has its bones outside its body.

○ **632**. Why do you close your mouth when you go under water ?

○ **633**. What kind of weather sometimes happens in the winter ?

○ **634**. Ask me a question that you don't know the answer to.

○ **635**. Do really smart people have a lot of questions too ?

○ **636**. Why do people take drugs ?

○ **637**. How do people communicate besides speaking ?

○ **638**. How do some animals communicate ?

○ **639**. Some babies are born, some people die. Is this a balance ?

○ **640**. What do you need if you go shopping ?

○ **641**. What should you do if you make a mess ?

○ **642**. What are some good fire safety tips ?

○ **643**. What does "freedom of speech" mean ?

○ **644**. What would you do if you found some pills ?

○ **645**. What is cheese made from ?

○ **646**. What do you find in the ocean besides fish ?

○ **647**. What things are too bright to safely look at ?

○ **648**. What are crayons and candles made of ?

○ **649**. How old will you be in 10 years ?

○ **650**. What does the moon go around ?

○ **651**. What does the earth go around ?

○ **652**. What comes out from the volcanoes ?

○ **653**. Where does the sun go at night ?

○ **654**. Who is taller, an ant or a bee ?

○ **655**. Who weighs more, Daddy or you ?

○ **656**. What do you say when the telephone rings ?

○ **657**. Why do people smoke ?

○ **658**. What country did your great-great grand parents come from ?

○ **659**. Are there some places on Earth that are not in a country ?

○ **660**. What would you do if you got lost in an amusement park ?

○ **661**. Where does bread come from ?

○ **662**. Why should you not stick something in an electrical outlet ?

○ **663**. What would happen if you ate only candy for dinner everyday ?

○ **664**. Where does pork come from ?

○ **665**. Where do rivers come from ?

666. Why do people read newspapers ?

667. What do you do that makes your parents proud ?

668. What do worms do in the ground ?

669. If you see a mushroom outside, should you eat it ?

670. If you had an apple tree in your yard, could you eat the apples ?

○ **671**. What is your favorite bedtime story ?

○ **672**. What do you do when you finish your chewing gum ?

○ **673**. Are there people inside a T.V. ?

○ **674**. Name five things that are not man-made.

○ **675**. Can you drink the water in a lake ?

○ **676**. Can you touch a rainbow ?

○ **677**. Can plants think ?

○ **678**. Can monkeys think ?

○ **679**. Who is older, someone 55 years old or someone 64 ?

○ **680**. What year is it ?

681. Why do alligators bite ?

682. What month is it ?

683. Who lives longer, flies or people ?

684. Who lives longer, most trees or most people ?

685. What happens to water when it gets very cold ?

A book to discover a child's imagination and knowledge

686. Can you hold your breath for one hour ?

687. Name some things on T.V. that are real.

688. How many numbers are there on a telephone ?

689. Do whales need to hold their breath a lot ?

690. Do all snakes bite ?

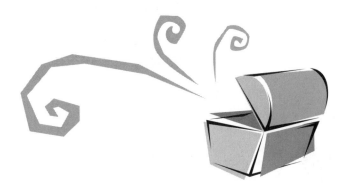

o **691**. Are some bugs dangerous ?

o **692**. Can getting sick sometimes be your fault ?

o **693**. Is getting sick always someone's fault ?

o **694**. Can a doctor prevent all sickness ?

o **695**. If you have four pieces of apple, and each piece is half an apple, how many whole apples would you have ?

○ **696**. What animals like to hop ?

○ **697**. What animals can sing ?

○ **698**. What animals can build a place to live ?

○ **699**. What do you like to pretend to be ?

○ **700**. Can you swim in ice ?

○ **701**. Is beer for kids ?

○ **702**. What drugs are okay for you to take ?

○ **703**. If there was a fire in your house and the door was locked, how could you get out ?

○ **704**. What makes you sad ?

○ **705**. What are some good ways you can protect your eyes ?

○ **706**. Are some boats only big enough for one person ?

○ **707**. Did people live 1,000 years ago ?

○ **708**. How old are your grandparents ?

○ **709**. Are all parents good parents ?

○ **710**. If someone does not get enough water, what can happen ?

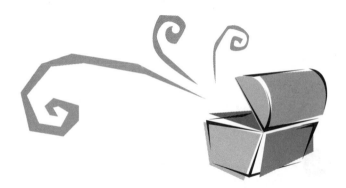

○ **711**. How do people make money ?

○ **712**. What does a bank do with money ?

○ **713**. Why should you save money ?

○ **714**. What things are worth a lot of money ?

○ **715**. What is worth more than money ?

A book to discover a child's imagination and knowledge

○ ***716***. Can you be replaced ?

○ ***717***. If you accidentally break something, what should you do ?

○ ***718***. Why is sharing a great thing ?

○ ***719***. What is the Internet ?

○ ***720***. Do you know how to turn a computer off ?

O **721**. What does a cow eat ?

O **722**. What goes in a camera ?

O **723**. After you take a picture, what do you need to do to get a picture you can see ?

O **724**. Should you always win ?

O **725**. Should you always try your best ?

○ **726**. Are all things in books real ?

○ **727**. Should you believe everything on T.V. ?

○ **728**. What is your skin for ?

○ **729**. Spell your teacher's name.

○ **730**. What kinds of nuts are there ?

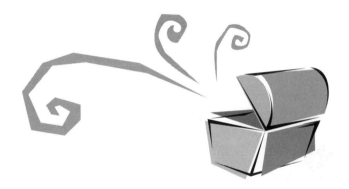

○ **731**. Should the clock on the
wall and a watch have the
same time ?

○ **732**. What would happen if you
did not wash your clothes ?

○ **733**. What are parents for ?

○ **734**. Can knives and guns be used
safely ?

○ **735**. What do horses do for
people ?

○ **736**. What are pets for ?

○ **737**. What are trains used for ?

○ **738**. What is the purpose of a hat ?

○ **739**. Why does a train sound its whistle ?

○ **740**. Name *four* things that are hot.

○ **741**. Name six things that are cold.

○ **742**. When should people wear a helmet ?

○ **743**. Can swimming be dangerous ? Why ?

○ **744**. What is your favorite family tradition ?

○ **745**. If you made two left turns, would you be going back where you came from ?

○ **746**. If you make four right turns, will you be going the same direction you are going now ?

○ **747**. Name some different kinds of jobs people can have.

○ **748**. Where would you like to go if you had enough time and enough money ?

○ **749**. If someone did something bad and told you not to tell, what would you do ?

○ **750**. Who loves you ?

○ **751**. Why do people eat ?

○ **752**. Can most birds walk ?

○ **753**. What is a good way to put out a campfire ?

○ **754**. What are some of the colors flowers can be ?

○ **755**. How long is a meter ?

A book to discover a child's imagination and knowledge

○ **756**. Are butterflies birds ?

○ **757**. Are bats a kind of bird ?

○ **758**. Is broken glass dangerous ?

○ **759**. What toys are good for your mind ?

○ **760**. What toys are good for babies but not for you ?

○ **761**. What do you need to go fishing ?

○ **762**. Why do you sometimes need life vests on a boat even if you know how to swim ?

○ **763**. Which is faster, running or swimming ?

○ **764**. Is there any food you like now, but you didn't like when you were younger ?

○ **765**. Can sound bounce ?

○ **766**. Should you be polite when you are at your friend's house ?

○ **767**. Where did you go on your last vacation ?

○ **768**. Name a place where have you not been but where you would like to go.

○ **769**. Can you think of something safe that looks dangerous ?

○ **770**. Can you think of something dangerous that looks safe ?

○ **771**. Do you feel safe at school ?

○ **772**. Can a computer make a person ?

○ **773**. Can a machine make a plant ?

○ **774**. Which is smarter, a newborn baby or a dog ?

○ **775**. What animals go to school ?

○ **776**. What is the biggest thing in the forest ?

○ **777**. Can you try your best even if something is really hard ?

○ **778**. Is there any way you can jump over a building ?

○ **779**. Can you do something that is impossible ?

○ **780**. Can a rock eat something ?

○ **781**. Can all questions be answered correctly with yes or no ?

○ **782**. Is everything in this world either good or bad ?

○ **783**. Can something that is good for one person be bad for others ?

○ **784**. Is it okay to do nothing at all sometimes ?

○ **785**. Can hard work be fun ?

○ **786**. Who is in your family ?

○ **787**. Is there any completely bad animal ?

○ **788**. Do teachers ever make mistakes ?

○ **789**. Is there an answer to every question ?

○ **790**. Describe an animal that is not real.

791. Name something that gets better when it gets older.

792. Which is better, new or fresh ?

793. Why do dogs like bones ?

794. Are sharks doing something bad when they eat fish ?

795. If you hear bad words, can you use them ?

○ **796**. What is your favorite amusement park ?

○ **797**. What are some good rules to follow ?

○ **798**. What material can light bounce off best ?

○ **799**. Where do you find people reading ?

○ **800**. Why are rivers sometimes dangerous ?

○ **801**. Are all vegetables green ?

○ **802**. Why are some vegetables green ?

○ **803**. Where is the nearest island ?

○ **804**. What is another way to explain who your cousin is ?

○ **805**. Is there any of your skin that never has any hair on it ?

○ **806**. What are some things you can do to make bicycling safe ?

○ **807**. Why is locking a car door important ?

○ **808**. Why should you not drink swimming pool water ?

○ **809**. Why should you not run around a swimming pool ?

○ **810**. What should you do if you think somebody needs help in the swimming pool ?

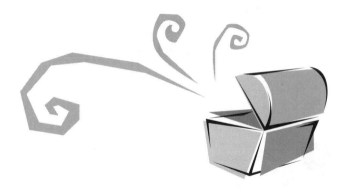

○ **811**. What is in the pool besides water ?

○ **812**. What is the color white made of ?

○ **813**. What kind of metals do you know ?

○ **814**. Are you sad if you kill a plant when you eat it ?

○ **815**. Do you need ice on the ground to skate ?

○ **816**. What do you need to swim ?

○ **817**. Do all birds eat worms ?

○ **818**. What happens to somebody if they get no exercise ?

○ **819**. What type of T.V. program is good for your mind ?

○ **820**. Name six things that are bad for your body.

○ **821**. Do cats have nine lives ?

○ **822**. Does any animal have more
than one life ?

○ **823**. Name 10 different ways to
exercise.

○ **824**. What color is a banana
before it is ripe ?

○ **825**. Do kittens come from any
other place besides a
mommy cat ?

○ **826**. Are you different from everyone else ?

○ **827**. Would the world be interesting if everyone were the same ?

○ **828**. Is your body made from the things you have eaten ?

○ **829**. Do you have a religion ?

○ **830**. Do some people have more than two eyes ?

○ **831**. Does everyone have feelings ?

○ **832**. Can animals feel pain ?

○ **833**. What are ice, snow and clouds all made of ?

○ **834**. Is your planet round ?

○ **835**. Is it a different time in some other countries ?

○ **836**. If it is daytime on this side of the planet, is it night time on the other side of the planet ?

○ **837**. What color is the earth ?

○ **838**. Is most of the earth made of water ?

○ **839**. Do you think there is life on other planets ?

○ **840**. Can you see animals from other planets in a museum ?

○ **841**. Is it always okay to kill animals ?

○ **842**. What do you feel like when you have a fever ?

○ **843**. If you have a cold, does it make you feel cold ?

○ **844**. Can you catch a cold if there are no germs ?

○ **845**. Are all germs bad ?

○ **846**. Do teachers know everything ?

○ **847**. When do you stop learning ?

○ **848**. Why do people pass gas ?

○ **849**. What might be funny but is something you should not laugh at ?

○ **850**. Name something that you can't see, but that you believe is real.

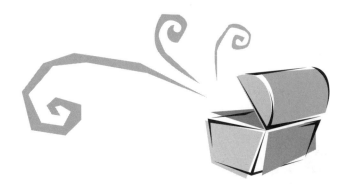

○ **851**. Why do most people eat animals ?

○ **852**. Why are some people fat ?

○ **853**. Is there any insect that is completely no good ?

○ **854**. Do you use math everyday ?

○ **855**. Who are Allah, Buddha, and Jesus ?

A book to discover a child's imagination and knowledge

○ **856**. Do you have a hobby ?

○ **857**. Where does paper come from ?

○ **858**. Where does thinking come from ?

○ **859**. Is getting dirty always bad ?

○ **860**. What do you do to make your parents happy ?

○ **861**. What is a second cousin, and do you have one ?

○ **862**. What is scary but not real ?

○ **863**. Are all vegetables good for you ?

○ **864**. What is your favorite book that is a true story ?

○ **865**. What is your favorite book that is not a true story ?

A book to discover a child's imagination and knowledge

○ **866**. What was the most embarrassing moment that has happened to you ?

○ **867**. Does most air have some water in it ?

○ **868**. Where do trees get their food ?

○ **869**. Do any plants eat people ?

○ **870**. Why do skunks stink ?

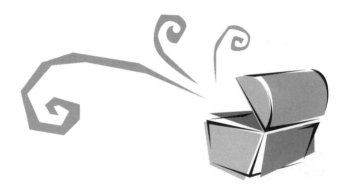

○ **871**. Can you walk on frozen water ?

○ **872**. Is it safe to walk on a frozen lake ?

○ **873**. What is an ice-skating rink made of ?

○ **874**. What are some of the things you can do to make you smarter ?

○ **875**. How do you feel if you hurt someone's feelings ?

A book to discover a child's imagination and knowledge

○ **876**. What do you do if someone calls you stupid ?

○ **877**. Why is it a bad idea to put your drink at the edge of a table ?

○ **878**. Why are two eyes better than one ?

○ **879**. Show me how long a foot is.

○ **880**. How many cards are in a deck of cards ?

○ **881**. If you drank three glasses of water everyday for three days, how many glasses would you drink ?

○ **882**. Does money grow on trees ?

○ **883**. What are some ways people earn money ?

○ **884**. If you could meet any person from history, who would you like to meet ?

○ **885**. Is there anything you can not buy with money ?

○ **886**. Who is no longer living in your family ?

○ **887**. How does your body change over time ?

○ **888**. Do you learn from your mistakes ?

○ **889**. What things are dangerous for your skin ?

○ **890**. How can you avoid being run over in the street ?

○ **891**. Are vampires real ?

○ **892**. What do mosquitoes eat ?

○ **893**. What do you eat that comes from the sea ?

○ **894**. Do you believe everything you read ?

○ **895**. Can some birds talk ?

A book to discover a child's imagination and knowledge

○ **896**. Can birds think like people ?

○ **897**. Do you make a lot of mistakes ?

○ **898**. Do you believe in Santa Claus ?

○ **899**. Why do people believe in something that is not real ?

○ **900**. What insects eat dead animals ?

○ **901**. What is in a lake but not in a swimming pool ?

○ **902**. What is a hot spring ?

○ **903**. Does a car use more gas going up hill or down hill ?

○ **904**. Can you learn more from books or from T.V. ?

○ **905**. What parts of the world are always cold ?

A book to discover a child's imagination and knowledge

○ **906**. In what parts of the world is it always wet ?

○ **907**. How many seconds can you hold your breath ?

○ **908**. How long can whales hold their breath ?

○ **909**. What is in air that our bodies need ?

○ **910**. What do our lungs do for us ?

○ **911**. What do fish do to get oxygen ?

○ **912**. Do all plants have leaves ?

○ **913**. Why is the sky blue ?

○ **914**. Name some birds that you have seen.

○ **915**. If you get angry, what are some ways to calm down ?

○ **916**. What animal eats bamboo shoots ?

○ **917**. Is air made of nitrogen and oxygen gasses ?

○ **918**. What other gasses do you know ?

○ **919**. If you don't know how to spell a word, how can you find out ?

○ **920**. If an animal's tail is cut off, can it grow a new one ?

○ **921**. Does the sun go around the earth ?

○ **922**. Does the moon go around the earth ?

○ **923**. How many planets are there in our solar system ?

○ **924**. Which is bigger, the moon, the sun or the earth ?

○ **925**. Are there people on the moon ?

926. Are there people living in space ?

927. Can you name some planets ?

928. Can cats see in the dark ?

929. Name some things that can hurt your ears.

930. What animal has the best eyesight ?

O **931**. Which animals are the smartest ?

O **932**. What are some differences between humans and apes ?

O **933**. Can some birds talk ?

O **934**. Can a small mistake kill you ?

O **935**. Where does a bed come from ?

○ **936**. What food stinks but tastes good ?

○ **937**. If a bracelet goes around your wrist and a necklace around your neck, what could go around your ankle ?

○ **938**. What should go on a dog's collar ?

○ **939**. Does your reflection look exactly like you ?

○ **940**. Can anyone read your mind ?

○ **941**. Name some animals that hibernate.

○ **942**. In the old days, what went in place of a bottle cap ?

○ **943**. Who came first, your mother or your grandmother ?

○ **944**. Which comes first, a tadpole or a frog ?

○ **945**. Can you always tell by looking at someone if they are friendly ?

946. Who is the boss of the house ?

947. Who is the boss of the toys ?

948. Where could you sleep in a city where you did not know anyone ?

949. What could be dangerous in a playground ?

950. Could something ever be good about an accident ?

951. Can you make up a nice name for a baby ?

952. What is something good about worms ?

953. What is something bad about kittens ?

954. What is the difference between radio and T.V. ?

955. What is the difference between a speaker and a microphone ?

A book to discover a child's imagination and knowledge

○ **956**. What can kids do that adults can't ?

○ **957**. What can newborn babies do that older kids can't ?

○ **958**. Why is dancing good for you ?

○ **959**. Is laughing good for you ?

○ **960**. Why do people cough ?

○ **961**. Can you name some colors that are not in the rainbow ?

○ **962**. Name something that costs no money but is very valuable.

○ **963**. Does the fire department close at night ?

○ **964**. What are police sirens for ?

○ **965**. Animals have skin. What do trees have ?

○ **966**. What can you do now to make your future better ?

○ **967**. What do dogs and trees have in common ?

○ **968**. What does it mean if a dog lies on its back ?

○ **969**. Are there more ants or people in the world ?

○ **970**. Name some countries that are islands.

971. Are all islands in the ocean ?

972. Is fighting sometimes necessary ?

973. Is it better to find fault in people or find some good in people ?

974. Name something good about someone you know who is usually bad.

975. Name something bad about someone you know who is usually good.

○ **976**. Is it okay to be dirty after digging in the mud ?

○ **977**. Why should a doctor clean up well before operating on someone ?

○ **978**. Why is dirt good for plants ?

○ **979**. What plants do you eat ?

○ **980**. What plants eat insects ?

○ **981**. If you could meet any character from a book you have read, who would you like to meet ?

○ **982**. Name something that smells good but is something you should not eat.

○ **983**. Is cooking only for girls ?

○ **984**. Should kids always be quiet ?

○ **985**. Should you always think before you speak ?

○ **986**. Can you make up a
confusing question ?

○ **987**. Are most stars older than
the earth ?

○ **988**. Is our sun just like other
stars, only closer ?

○ **989**. If you have a private
question, who can you ask,
besides your parents ?

○ **990**. Do people sometimes talk
but have nothing to say ?

○ **991**. Do all Chinese people live in China ?

○ **992**. What came first, the chicken or the egg ?

○ **993**. About how many hours do you sleep at night ?

○ **994**. What are some ways you can be nice to people ?

○ **995**. When is it okay to play on a street ?

○ ***996***. What hurts, falling or landing ?

○ ***997***. What fruit has its seeds on the outside ?

○ ***998***. What is the longest word you can spell ?

○ ***999***. What two words only have one letter ?

○ ***1000***. Can you think of a question that no one can answer ?

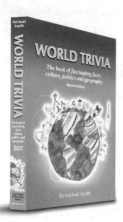

World Trivia

The book of fascinating facts: culture, politics and geography
By Michael Smith

"A fat little volume full of little known facts from around the world."

—— Today's Librarian

"It contains an excellent selection of questions that I found genuinely interesting."

—— Harold McFarland, Editor, Readers Preference Reviews

World Trivia reveals many amazing and amusing facts of culture, politics and geography. Distinctly different from most trivia books, it illustrates a broad range of cultures and political realities. It is designed to challenge even the most knowledgeable, and to enrich our knowledge of the world and its people. This book is for all readers, especially those thinking globally.

About the Author:

Michael Smith is a real traveler. At recent count, he has been to more than 70 different countries, where he has learned about cultures by immersing himself in them. He is also a frequent lecturer on budget travel.

Trivia/Social Studies/Game/Reference
ISBN: 0966943724, Price: $9.95, Size: 5" x 7.25", Paperback, 268 pages

Publisher edition: $9.95

East West Discovery Press

P.O. Box 2393, Gardena, CA 90247.
Phone (310)532-1115 / Fax (310)768-8926